BACHARACH AND DAVID
5 MODERN CLASSICS ARRANGED BY PHILLIP KEVEREN

CONTENTS

— PIANO LEVEL —
LATE INTERMEDIATE/EARLY ADVANCED

ISBN 978-1-4584-1508-0

HAL•LEONARD®
CORPORATION

7777 W. BLUEMOUND RD. P.O. BOX 13819 MILWAUKEE, WI 53213

Visit Hal Leonard Online at
www.halleonard.com

Visit Phillip at
www.phillipkeveren.com

PREFACE

The collaboration of Burt Bacharach and Hal David resulted in some of the most enduring popular music of the 20th century. Hal's lyrics are witty, whimsical, and warm. Burt's music is full of rhythmic surprises, catchy melodies, and sophisticated harmonies. The songs that emerge create a body of work that is completely unique in the pop canon.

In approaching these solo piano arrangements, I did not try to imitate any particular recordings exclusively. Although many of these songs are strongly connected to a particular artist, (Dionne Warwick, B.J. Thomas, Herb Alpert, et al.), each composition has been interpreted by myriad artists through the years. My settings tend to highlight the jazz leanings that are a common thread through all of Mr. Bacharach's work.

One of the first books I remember owning was *The Bacharach and David Songbook*. In my first year of school at Mount Hood Community College (Gresham, Oregon), I decided to try my hand at arranging for the vocal jazz ensemble. My first attempt was "Alfie." I later adapted this arrangement for the jazz band as well. Not long after that "The Look of Love" found itself shoehorned into a 5/4 setting. I'm not sure that worked so well, but I learned a lot about arranging in the process! All that to say: I am a longtime admirer of the songs Bacharach and David gave the world.

Sincerely,

Phillip Keveren

BIOGRAPHY

Phillip Keveren, a multi-talented keyboard artist and composer, has composed original works in a variety of genres from piano solo to symphonic orchestra. Mr. Keveren gives frequent concerts and workshops for teachers and their students in the United States, Canada, Europe, and Asia. Mr. Keveren holds a B.M. in composition from California State University Northridge and a M.M. in composition from the University of Southern California.

ALFIE
Theme from the Paramount Picture ALFIE

Words by HAL DAVID
Music by BURT BACHARACH
Arranged by Phillip Keveren

Slowly, with rubato (♩ = c. 60)

ANYONE WHO HAD A HEART

Lyric by HAL DAVID
Music by BURT BACHARACH
Arranged by Phillip Keveren

Very slowly and steadily ($\.= 52$)

With pedal

DO YOU KNOW THE WAY TO SAN JOSE

Lyric by HAL DAVID
Music by BURT BACHARACH
Arranged by Phillip Keveren

A HOUSE IS NOT A HOME

Lyric by HAL DAVID
Music by BURT BACHARACH
Arranged by Phillip Keveren

Expressively (♩ = 66-72)

With pedal

I'LL NEVER FALL IN LOVE AGAIN
from PROMISES, PROMISES

Lyric by HAL DAVID
Music by BURT BACHARACH
Arranged by Phillip Keveren

Flowing (♩ = 126-132)

I SAY A LITTLE PRAYER

Lyric by HAL DAVID
Music by BURT BACHARACH
Arranged by Phillip Keveren

With pedal

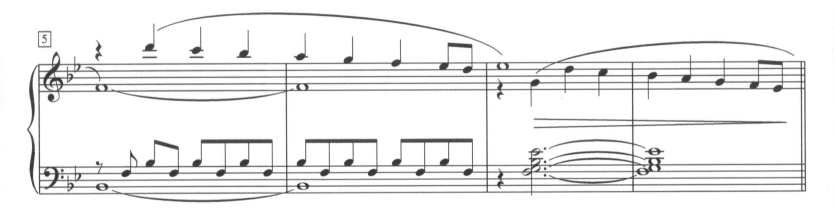

THE LOOK OF LOVE
from CASINO ROYALE

Words by HAL DAVID
Music by BURT BACHARACH
Arranged by Phillip Keveren

Dreamily (♩ = 100)

MAGIC MOMENTS

Lyric by HAL DAVID
Music by BURT BACHARACH
Arranged by Phillip Keveren

Lighthearted (♩. = 96)

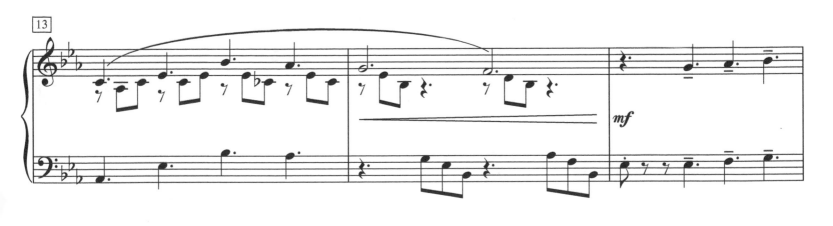

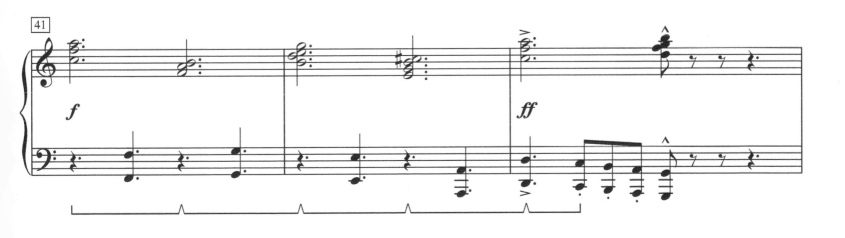

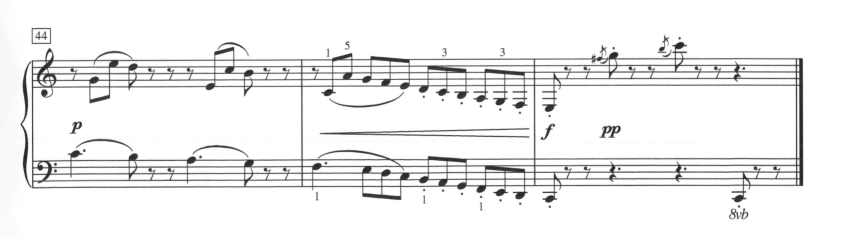

ONE LESS BELL TO ANSWER

Lyric by HAL DAVID
Music by BURT BACHARACH
Arranged by Phillip Keveren

RAINDROPS KEEP FALLIN' ON MY HEAD
from BUTCH CASSIDY AND THE SUNDANCE KID

Lyric by HAL DAVID
Music by BURT BACHARACH
Arranged by Phillip Keveren

THIS GUY'S IN LOVE WITH YOU

Lyric by HAL DAVID
Music by BURT BACHARACH
Arranged by Phillip Keveren

40

WALK ON BY

Lyric by HAL DAVID
Music by BURT BACHARACH
Arranged by Phillip Keveren

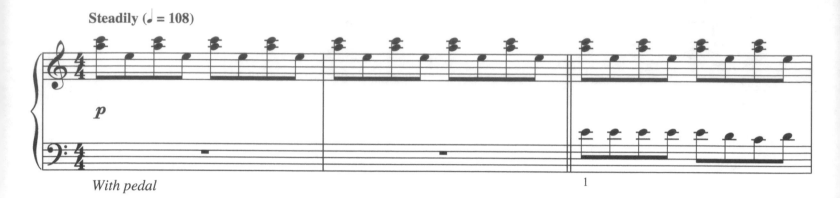

WISHIN' AND HOPIN'

Lyric by HAL DAVID
Music by BURT BACHARACH
Arranged by Phillip Keveren

WHAT THE WORLD NEEDS NOW IS LOVE

Lyric by HAL DAVID
Music by BURT BACHARACH
Arranged by Phillip Keveren

WIVES AND LOVERS

(Hey, Little Girl)

from the Paramount Picture WIVES AND LOVERS

Words by HAL DAVID
Music by BURT BACHARACH
Arranged by Phillip Keveren

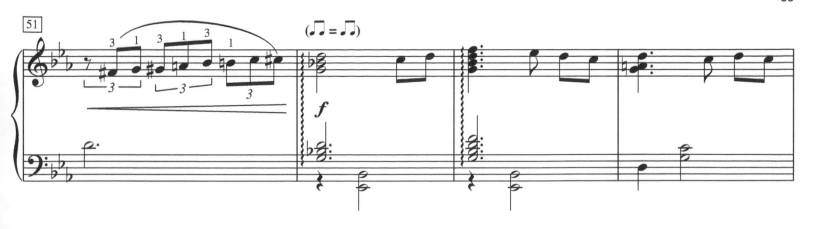

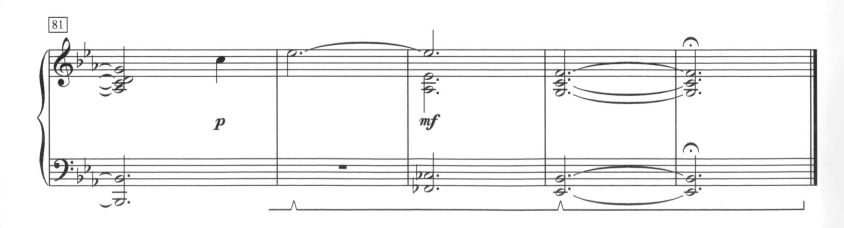